For Dec 25, 2003

Kim

From Maxine With Love

TEACH YOUR CHILDREN WELL

By Evelyn Loeb and Virginia Unser

Illustrated by C. James Frazier

PETER PAUPER PRESS, INC.
WHITE PLAINS, NEW YORK

*For our children
and our children's children*

Text copyright © 1998
Peter Pauper Press, Inc.
202 Mamaroneck Avenue
White Plains, NY 10601
All rights reserved
ISBN 0-88088-896-2
Printed in China
7 6 5 4 3 2 1

Introduction

*T*reat others as you would like to be treated; beauty is present in all living things; giving enriches the giver as much as the recipient. Even the youngest child can appreciate these universal lessons. Children learn by example, and it is up to us to serve as models for them to emulate. It is as important to nourish children spiritually as it is to feed their growing bodies.

It is one of life's great joys to watch children develop, both physically and emotionally. It is also a privilege to reveal to them some of life's greatest pleasures: a starry sky, a loving touch, a shared meal. In turn, children give back to us their love and laughter, and can teach us how to look at the world with "new" eyes.

Teach your children well, and we will all be enriched.

E. L. and V. U.

Teach Your Children Well

—— ≈ ——

An act of kindness
is an act of love.

≈

Treat a child gently and you will
teach compassion.

Teach Your Children Well

When you
speak softly
you are more apt
to be heard.

Teach Your Children Well

Eat together
and your children will learn
not only manners but also
the meaning of family.

Teach Your Children Well

Think before you speak;
it is easier to forget
what was never said.

Teach Your Children Well

~

Praise gets more attention
than blame.

~

A loving touch can often erase
a foolish remark.

*P*lay together.
The sound
of laughter
is never
forgotten.

Teach Your Children Well

~

Working side by side
you teach by example.

~

Teach your children well.
Your grandchildren will be
the beneficiaries of your
love and wisdom.

Teach Your Children Well

———— ∼ ————

When you
share the fruits of your labor,
your children will know
the meaning of charity.

Teach Your Children Well

*I*t is easier
to forgive
than to hold
a grudge.

Teach Your Children Well

～

Set a good example
by forgiving those who
have wronged you.

～

If you're bored, you're boring.

*S*hare your
hopes and dreams
with your children,
and truly they will
hope and dream as well.

Teach Your Children Well

— ~ —

Take trips together.
When you play together,
you stay together.

~

Accept imperfections;
even the sky is sometimes
filled with clouds.

Teach Your Children Well

~

There are often two sides
to a story. One person's poison is
another person's ambrosia.

~

If you support a leaning tree
it will continue to shade you
from the sun.

*Take a deep breath
and smell the roses.
Down the road
the air might not
smell so sweet.*

Teach Your Children Well

═══ ~ ═══

A problem solved is
no longer a problem.

~

Helping hands are
beautiful hands.

Teach Your Children Well

———— ≈ ————

$\mathscr{D}$o the best you can.
Perfection and happiness
don't necessarily go
hand in hand.

*A*llow your children
to see you make a mistake.
They need to know that
you are human, too.

Teach Your Children Well

═══ ∼ ═══

*B*e lavish with hugs and kisses.
There is no such thing as
too much affection.

∼

*L*ove unconditionally.
It's contagious!

Teach Your Children Well

— ∽ —

Set high standards. Your children
will rise to meet them.

∽

Choose sweet words;
you may have to
eat them.

*I*f you count stars
with your children,
they will discover the
magnificence
of the heavens.

Teach Your Children Well

---~---

Teaching is a two-way street.
Learn from your children.

~

Acts of kindness are never
isolated incidents. They connect us
all in the circle of life.

Teach Your Children Well

—— ≈ ——

If you can laugh at yourself,
you have taken a step on the
road to enlightenment.

≈

There is dignity and beauty
at every stage of life.

Teach Your Children Well

=～=

Embrace the grand tapestry of life.
You are weaving a little square
of the future.

～

Make time to marvel at a flower,
or the snowflakes.

Teach Your Children Well

―――∽―――

Teach your children the beauty
of a rainy day.

∽

Take the scenic route
once in a while. Your children
will enjoy the journey.

Teach Your Children Well

～

Love and laughter
turn a "house" into a "home."

～

Your children will soar if you act
as their safety net.

Teach Your Children Well

———— ∾ ————

If you take risks, your children
will learn courage.

∾

The best hugs start with
two people and radiate outward.

Teach Your Children Well

See the world
through your children's eyes.
To them, everything is
new and wonderful.

Teach Your Children Well

———— ～ ————

Extend yourself for other people,
and your children will learn to go
the "extra mile."

～

The gift of yourself
far outshines anything that could
be found in a store.

Teach Your Children Well

--- ~ ---

*E*veryone has special talents.
Help your children
to discover their own,
and make the most of them.

*T*here is
as much beauty
in the caterpillar
as in the butterfly.

Teach Your Children Well

═══ ～ ═══

Treat your children fairly,
and they will learn
to be just.

～

The root of "discipline" is:
"to teach."

Teach Your Children Well

~

Cookies baked by loving hands
taste the best.

~

Be generous with
encouragement and
sparing with criticism.

Nobody ever
learned anything
without
making mistakes.

Teach Your Children Well

*R*espect your
children's opinions ...
and they will gain
self-confidence.

When your children stumble, dust them off and encourage them to try again.